I want to acknowledge and thank my amazing mom for her invaluable help in editing my stories, as well as my dad for his belief in me and support in making my dream of being a writer a reality.

My little brother has been a source of inspiration for my stories, and I am grateful for his support. Special thanks to Maimuna and Abdullahi for their unwavering support, and to the illustrator for breathing life into my characters. You all hold a special place in my heart, and I am grateful for your contributions to my success as a writer.

To my dear readers,
This book is dedicated to all those who have faced discrimination and bullying because of their race, religion or background. I hope that through the pages of this book, you find the courage and inspiration to stand up against injustice and embrace diversity. You are not alone, and your voice matters.

Little Lee was so lonely. He had nothing to do but look out the window and watch kids playing. He couldn't go outside, ... Especially because of all those bullies that do nothing but tease little Lee. Being an immigrant from Ukraine, it was routine... in this country to find someone from Ukraine and remind them of how weak they are.

When Little Lee bothered to go outside, he would think of one torture after another. Kids would pull his ears and say, "You're a loser, Lee!" or grab his little teddy and say, "You're a numbskull!" and then run away laughing.

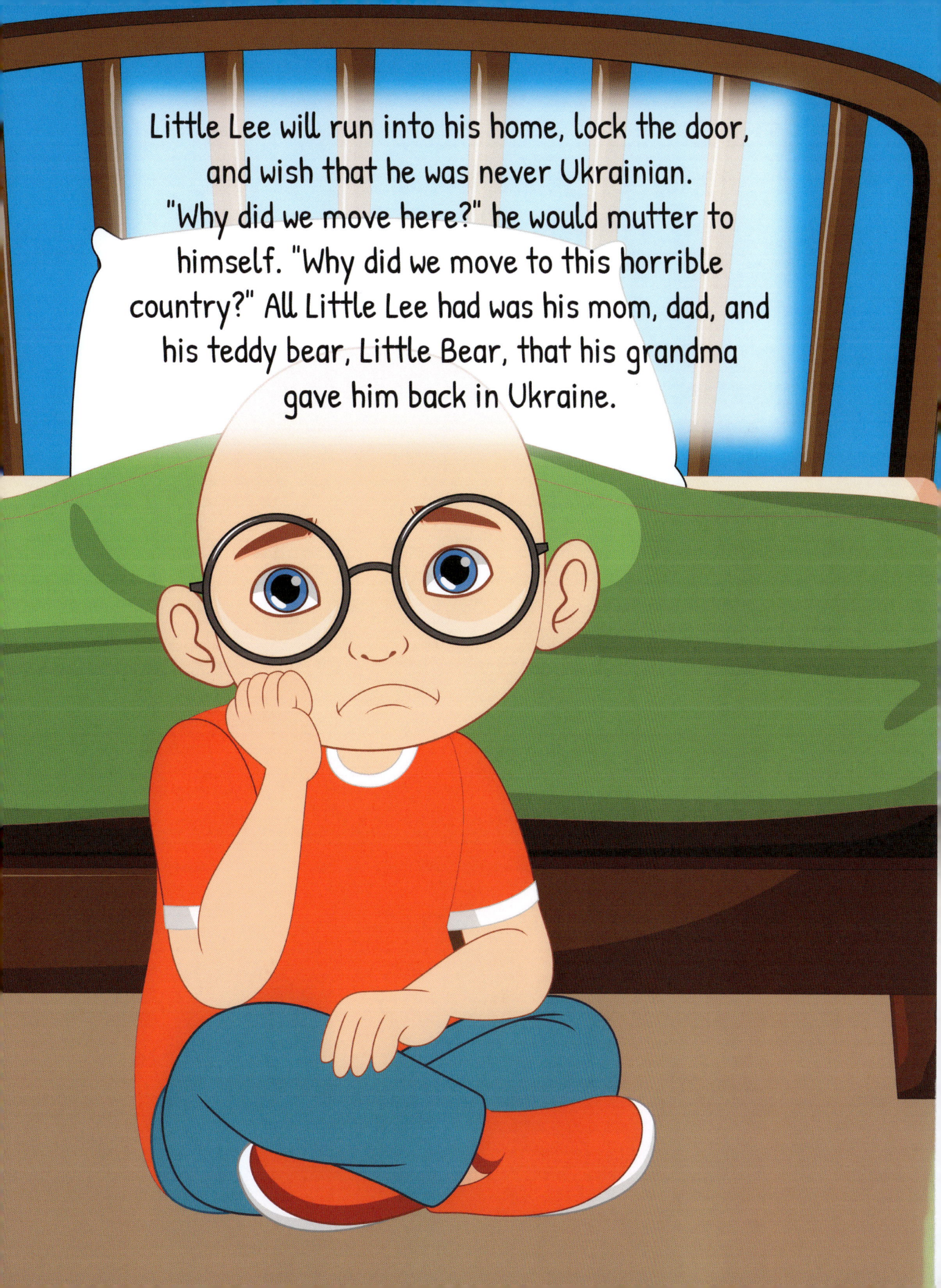

Little Lee will run into his home, lock the door, and wish that he was never Ukrainian. "Why did we move here?" he would mutter to himself. "Why did we move to this horrible country?" All Little Lee had was his mom, dad, and his teddy bear, Little Bear, that his grandma gave him back in Ukraine.

Then one day, after a miserable day of bullying, Little Lee decided to go fishing. He loved fishing, so he went out to a lake, got his fishing rod, and started fishing. As he was fishing, he felt a bite. He grabbed his rod and pulled!

He pulled!, pulled! and pulled!

Until finally, he got something. He looked at the thing he had caught. IT WAS A SNAPPER! Slowly, the snapper began to talk.
"Hi, Little Lee! How are you?" It asked as Little Lee stared at it with curious eyes.
"How do you know my name?" Little Lee asked, holding onto his rod.

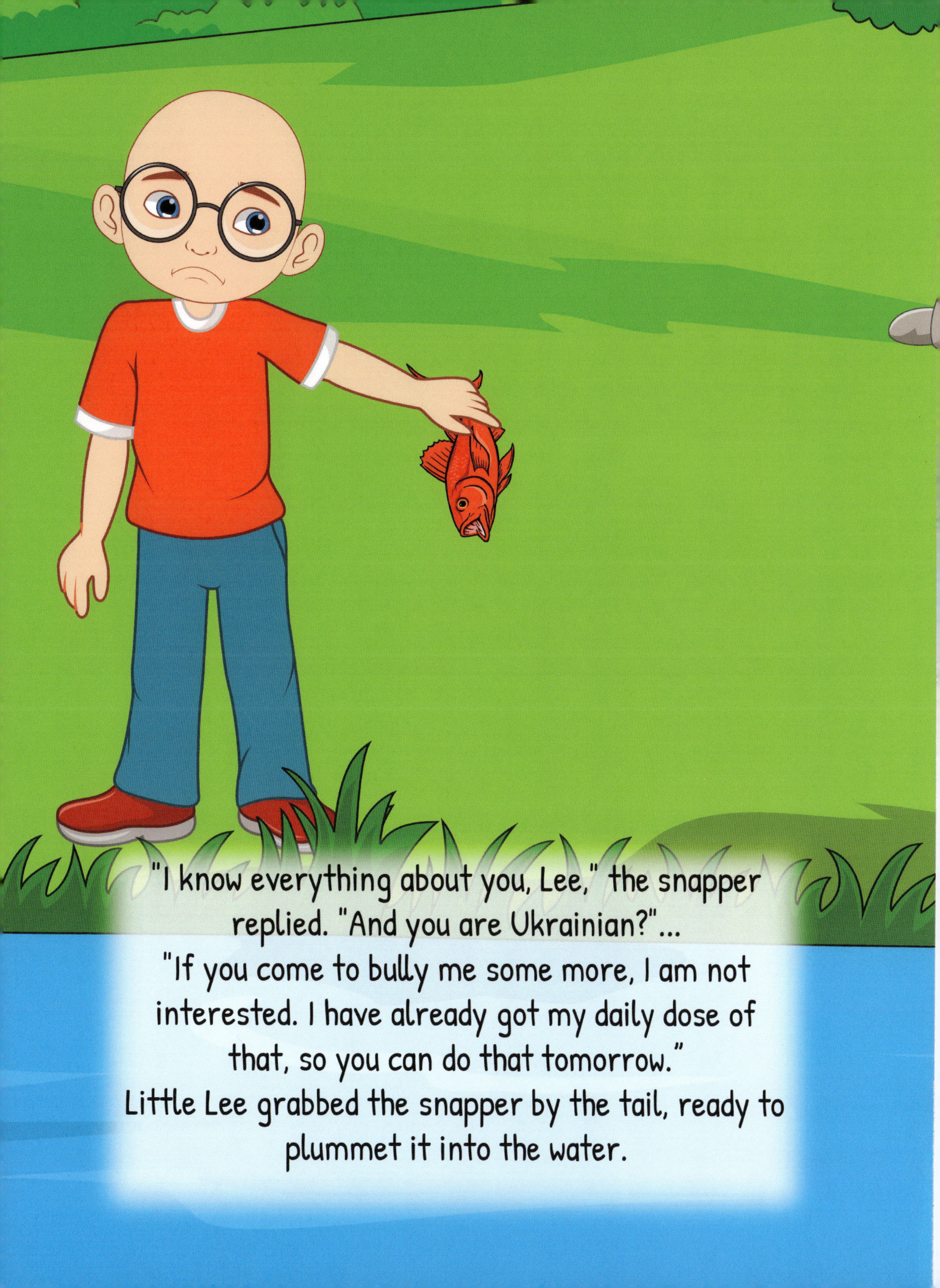

"I know everything about you, Lee," the snapper replied. "And you are Ukrainian?"...
"If you come to bully me some more, I am not interested. I have already got my daily dose of that, so you can do that tomorrow."
Little Lee grabbed the snapper by the tail, ready to plummet it into the water.

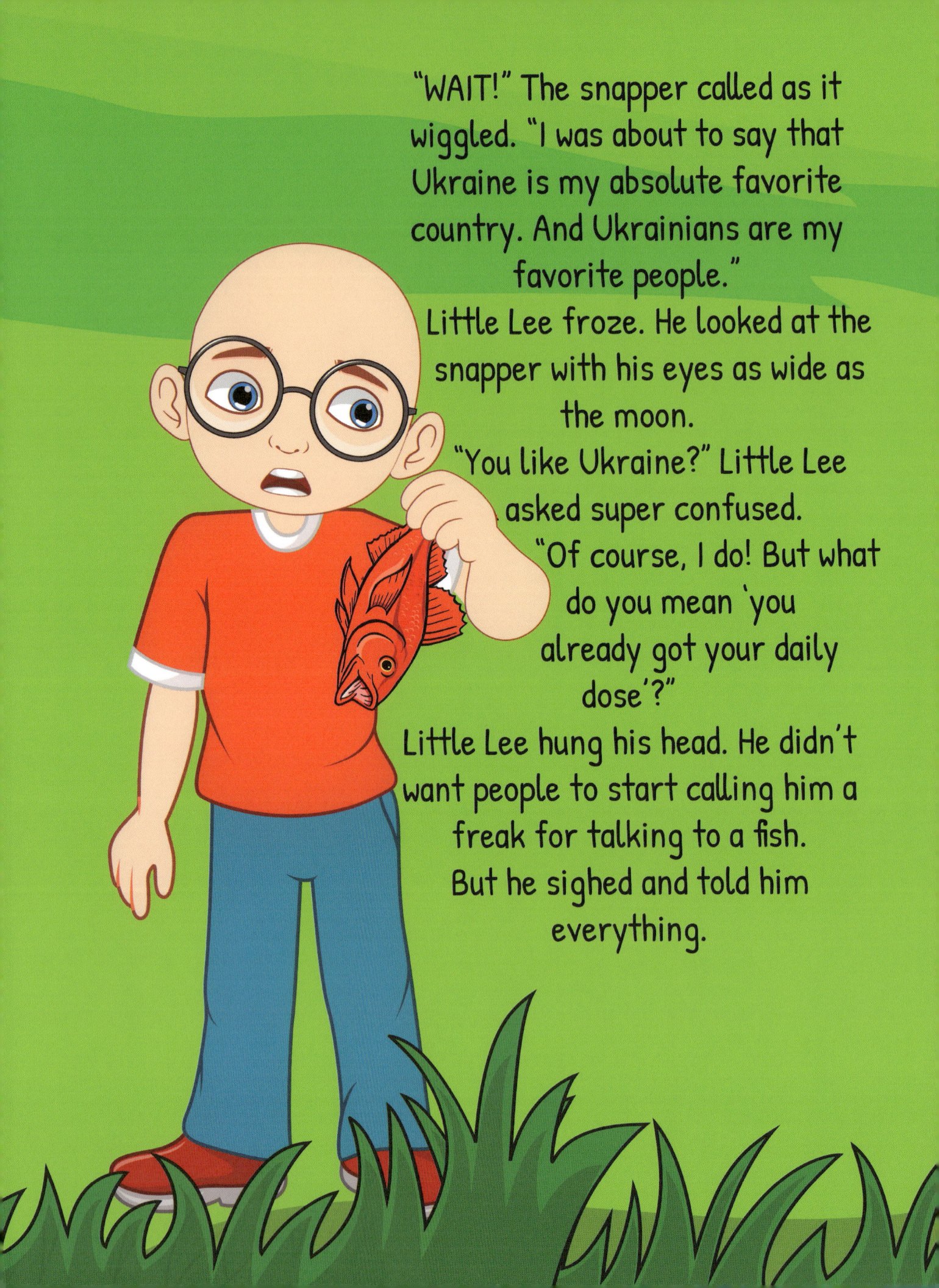

"WAIT!" The snapper called as it wiggled. "I was about to say that Ukraine is my absolute favorite country. And Ukrainians are my favorite people."

Little Lee froze. He looked at the snapper with his eyes as wide as the moon.

"You like Ukraine?" Little Lee asked super confused.

"Of course, I do! But what do you mean 'you already got your daily dose'?"

Little Lee hung his head. He didn't want people to start calling him a freak for talking to a fish.

But he sighed and told him everything.

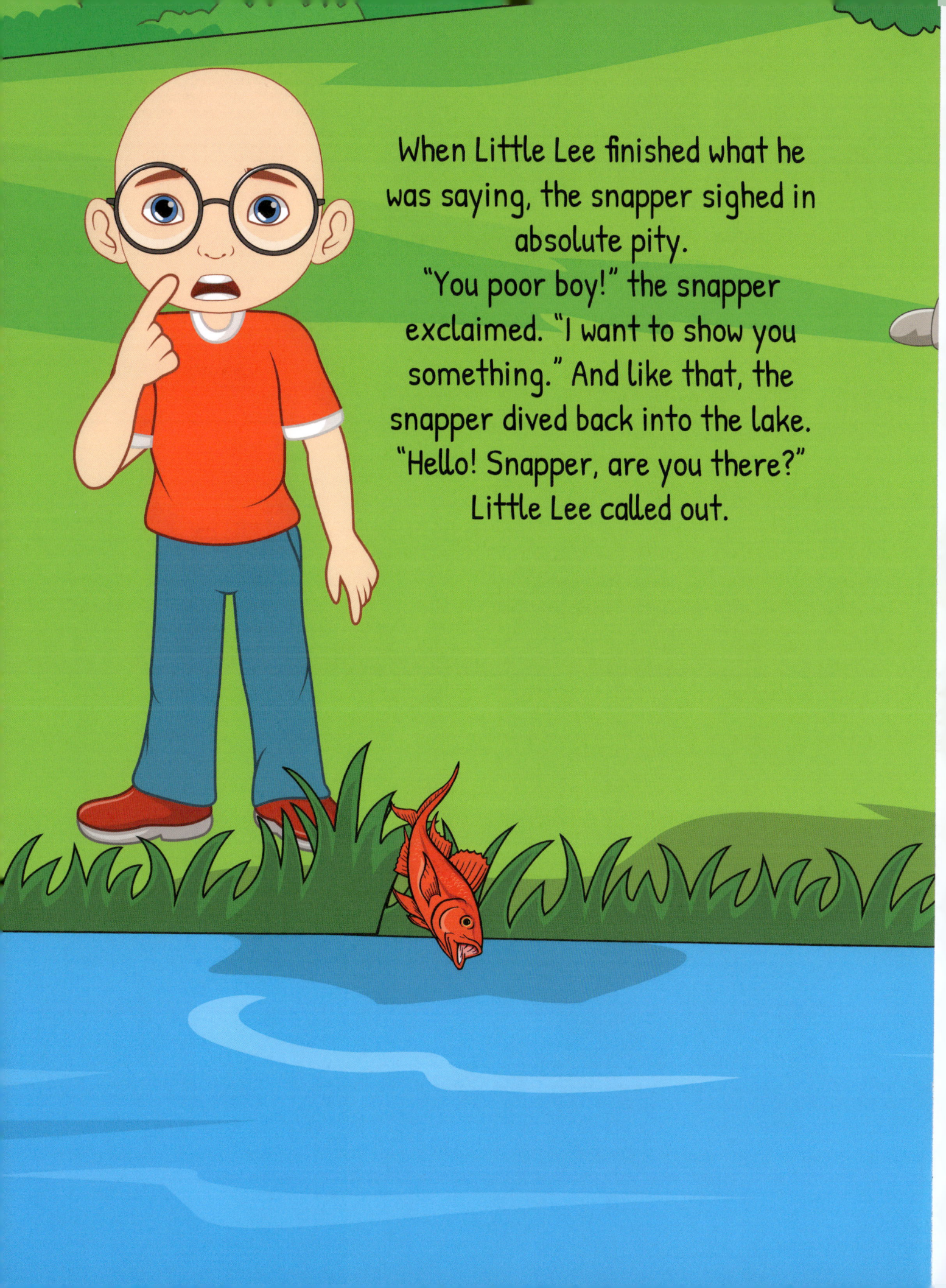

When Little Lee finished what he was saying, the snapper sighed in absolute pity.
"You poor boy!" the snapper exclaimed. "I want to show you something." And like that, the snapper dived back into the lake.
"Hello! Snapper, are you there?" Little Lee called out.

But the Snapper was nowhere to be seen. Little Lee sighed and was about to go back to his house. As he continued walking, he accidentally slipped on the rocks and fell into the water! SPLASH!!!

Little Lee cried and struggled until he realized... He could breathe under the water. Little Lee bobbed in the water in shock of what had happened, until he caught the eye of the Snapper. He swam after it.

Little Lee was zigzagging left and right to catch up to the snapper. But as he was going, he saw the wonders of the sea. He saw beautiful fish and whales playing and swimming. He saw marine animals swimming in circles around him, wondering who the person was that had come into their ocean.

"Do you like them?" The snapper asked as he saw Little Lee playing with the colorful creatures.
"I do! I wish I was like them," Little Lee sighed, remembering all the horrible bullying.
"But you are like them!" The snapper exclaimed.
"I am?" Little Lee asked.

"Follow me!"
And Little Lee and the snapper continued to swim through the beautiful ocean.

Little Lee and the snapper swam until a horrible stench filled the ocean.
"Ewww!!" Little Lee said. "What's that smell?"
The snapper pointed its tail towards the dog poop on the ocean floor. Beautiful sea animals were swimming above the poop peacefully.

"You see those sea animals? You are like them," the snapper said. "LIKE THEM! I am not a marine animal!" Little Lee laughed.
"You aren't like them on the outside, but you are like them on the inside. Your heart is beautiful, majestic and peaceful just like them."
"I guess I never thought of it that way," Little Lee said in awe.

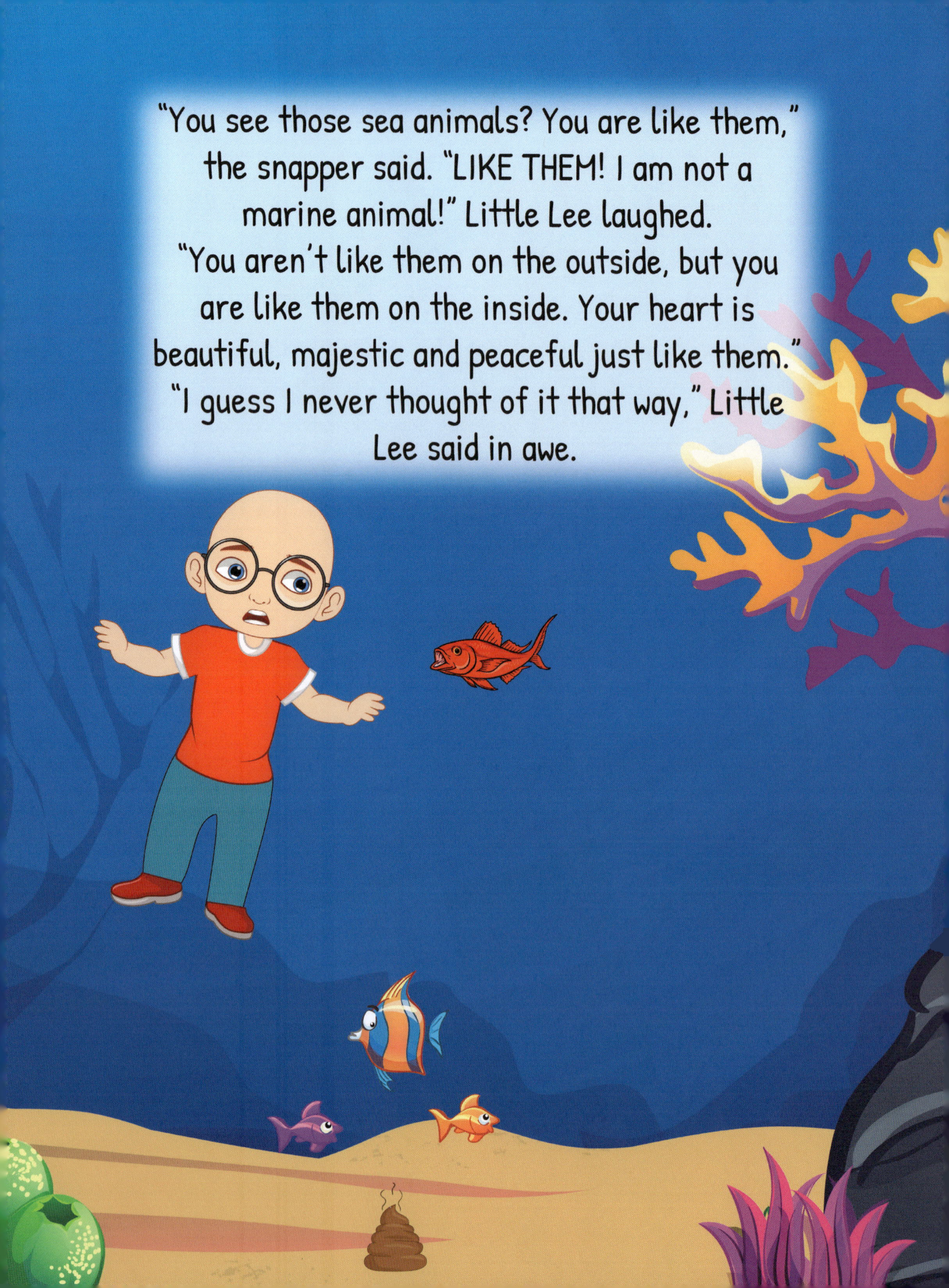

"You see that jellyfish?" the snapper asked, pointing its tail at the lilac-colored jellyfish. "Yeah!" Little Lee replied.
"You're just like that jellyfish, majestic and peaceful."
"I am! Wow!."
"But there's one thing that a jellyfish can do that you can't." "What is that?" Little Lee asked.
"You see that dog poop? Those are the bullies."
"THEY ARE?" Little Lee asked.
"They are! You see, you are always running away from the bullies. But that jellyfish is going over them."

"What are you saying?" Little Lee asked.
"I am saying, compared to those bullies, you are better than them. You are a majestic jellyfish! They are a piece of poop. Why would you be afraid of poop, when you can simply walk over it?"
"You're right!" Little Lee said.

"Exactly! When you learn to step over those bullies, then you will become a true jellyfish." Little Lee watched as the jellyfish harmlessly floated over the dog poop like it was nothing. Little Lee decided that was who he wanted to be.

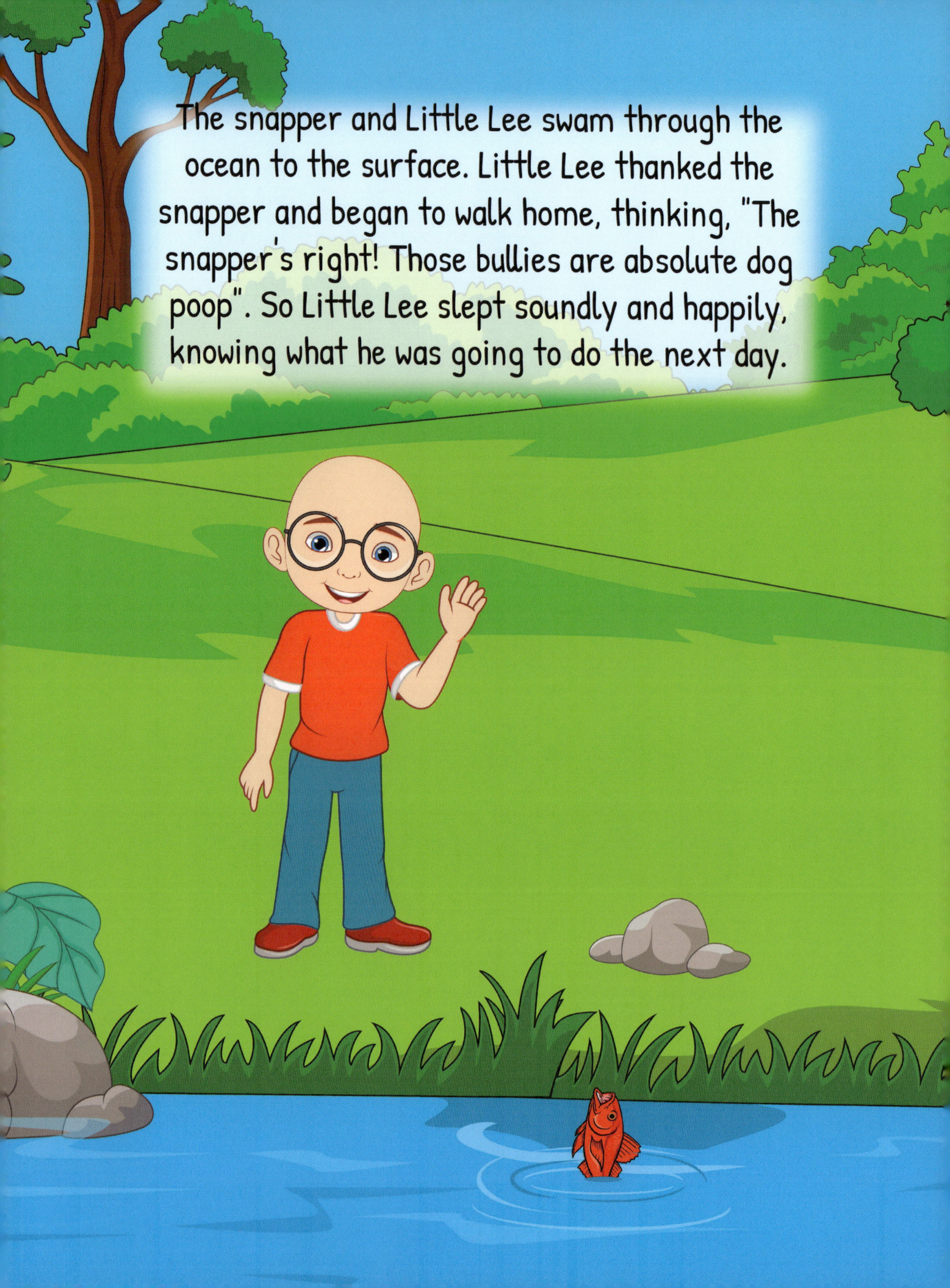

The snapper and Little Lee swam through the ocean to the surface. Little Lee thanked the snapper and began to walk home, thinking, "The snapper's right! Those bullies are absolute dog poop". So Little Lee slept soundly and happily, knowing what he was going to do the next day.

The next day when the bullies struck, instead of Little Lee crying, he pretended the bullies weren't there and continued walking.

"Hey Lee, you brainless loser! Come here!" They shouted, but Little Lee simply pictured the bullies as dog poop and continue walking. The bullies were shocked that they could no longer mess with Little Lee, and if anyone did, he would think to himself: "I am a jellyfish, I am not weak," and continued playing.

When the bullies stopped harassing Lee, a young Ukrainian girl approached Lee and asked, "How do you manage to cope with the bullying so well?" she asked eagerly. Lee replied by saying,

Let's just say I'm a jellyfish that can float over dog poop.

THE END

What type of marine animal are you?